CINDY ANN PITTS

This Book Belongs to:

____

LifeWay Press
127 Ninth Avenue, North
Nashville, Tennessee

Nashville, Tennessee
7200-17

Dewey Decimal Classification Number 306.874
Subject Heading: Children of Divorced Parents
Printed in the United States of America

Children/Preschool Section
Youth/Children/Preschool Department
Discipleship and Family Development Division
The Sunday School Board of the Southern Baptist Convention
127 Ninth Avenue, North
Nashville, Tennessee 37234

To the children who have truly been
my teachers at Plymouth Park Baptist Church (1981-1984) and
Houston's First Baptist Church (1984-present).

Contents

Getting to Know You

1. What name do you like your friends to call you? ____________________

2. Do you have any pets? If yes, what kind and what are their names? ____________________

____

3. What is your favorite subject in school? ____________________

4. What is your favorite flavor of ice cream? ____________________

5. Do you collect anything? If so, what? ____________________

6. What do you like to do just for fun? ____________________

I Can Be a Promise Keeper

I promise to keep in confidence all the personal information anyone shares during our KidShare group time. I understand that the only personal information I can share about our group is what I say. I will not talk about what other group members share.

____

(my signature)

My group members also promise to keep in confidence what I share.

____________________ ____________________

____________________ ____________________

____________________ ____________________

____________________ ____________________

GOD MADE ME

Did you know that everyone has a unique (that means one of a kind) set of fingerprints? God is very creative! He has so many ideas. He does not have to repeat them. He did not make any two people alike. No, not even identical twins are really identical. You are a creation of God.

My favorite fun thing to do is

My Fingerprint

My hair color is

I want to be called

I go to______________________

______________________School

My favorite candy is

____

My favorite color is

____

"I am fearfully and wonderfully made" *(Psalm 139:14)*

Designer Made

"So God created man in his own image, in the image of God he created him; male and female he created them" *(Genesis 1:27)*.

Being made in God's image means we are like God in some ways.

Fill in the blanks below to help you discover how we are made in God's image.

know **love** **plan** **communicate** **talk** **choices** **think**

I am like God because . . .

1. I can _____________ with God.
2. I can _____________ right from wrong.
3. I can make _____________.
4. I can _____________ and _____________.
5. I can _____________ with other people.
6. I can _____________ God and others.
7. I can feel love, joy, sorrow, disappointment, and hope. God gave me feelings. Circle some of the feelings that you have experienced this week.

Excited	**Tired**	**Afraid**	**Glad**
Calm	**Surprised**	**Bored**	**Lonely**
Angry	**Lazy**	**Confused**	**Happy**
Discouraged	**Cheerful**	**Silly**	**Cared About**

Even though God made billions of people on earth, He knows you by name. The God who made you loves you — He even likes you!

God Knows How I Feel

DENIAL

THIS CAN'T BE HAPPENING TO ME!

There are times we get news so unpleasant that we wish it were not true. For a while our minds will tell us, "No, this can't be happening to me!" When our feelings say no to what is really happening, we are in a stage of grief called *denial.*

For a brief time, denial may help us to adjust to what has happened. We should not stay in denial for long. We have to look honestly at our situation so that we can make good decisions. We need to decide how we can best react to the changes in our lives. Pretending the unpleasant or sad events did not happen will not help us.

Below are examples of times that children your age may have feelings of denial. See if you can name others.

1. You learn your parents are going to get a divorce.

2. You learn your dad is going to remarry.

3. You learn your mother, who remarried last year, is going to have a new baby. The new baby will have the same last name of your mother and stepfather.

4. You learn____

   ____.

5. You learn____

   ____.

Thinking Back

1. The way I learned about my parents' divorce was ______________________________

   ____

   ____

2. The feelings I remember having were ______________________________

   ____

   ____

3. What I really wanted to say to my parents was ______________________________

   ____

   ____

4. Most of all, I feared ______________________________

   ____

   ____

5. When I am afraid, my body feels ______________________________

   ____

6. I usually react by ______________________________

   ____

"Cast all your anxiety on him because he cares for you" *(I Peter 5:7).*

Anger

Sometimes I Just Feel So Angry

Anger is one of the five basic feelings all people have. Everyone gets angry from time to time. Feelings are not right or wrong. (Feelings are just feelings!)

There are good reasons for feeling angry. There are times we are angry because we know of someone who is not being treated fairly. Our anger should make us want to help them. If our anger causes us to want to do something right and good, it is the good kind of anger.

The Bible tells us about a time Jesus became angry. He was angry because merchants were selling things in the temple. Instead of charging fair prices these merchants were charging too much. They were taking advantage of poor people, and this made Jesus angry. He sent the merchants out of the temple. He said, "'My house will be called a house of prayer,' but you are making it a 'den of robbers'" (Matthew 21:13). We can also feel anger for the wrong reasons. This can happen at times when we are selfish and are angry only because we want our own way. If our anger makes us want to hurt ourselves or other people, we are angry for the wrong reasons.

We can choose how we react to angry feelings. In this session we are going to learn new ways of reacting to anger. We are going to think about why we feel angry and learn some good ways to handle our feelings.

It Just Makes Me So Angry

1. ______________________________

2. ______________________________

3. ______________________________

4. ______________________________

5. ______________________________

6. ______________________________

____

When I am angry, I usually ______________________________

____

____

Listed below are some ways angry people react. Circle some things you have done when you were angry.

1. Scream/Yell
2. Avoid people (want to be alone)
3. Hit others
4. Throw things
5. Cry
6. Say mean things to others
7. Cannot sleep
8. Feel sick (head or stomach)
9. Frown
10. Kick
11. Stomp feet
12. Cross arms

Positive Ways to Handle Anger

1. Talk about it.

2. Exercise.

3. Count to 100! (or more)

4. Remove yourself from the situation.

5. Take time out to do something you enjoy or that will relax you until you calm down.
   Good Examples:
   - ♡ read a book
   - ♡ take a bubble bath
   - ♡ play a computer game
   - ♡ listen to music
   - ♡ paint or draw
   - ♡ work on your favorite hobby

6. Write your feelings down on paper.

7. List the choices you have.

Remember, you still have to deal with your anger. Think about why you are angry and talk to people who can help you. Decide what can be done to change or improve the situation that made you angry.

What can you do?

1. ____

   ____

2. ____

   ____

Think About Your Anger

Think back to the last time you were angry. What made you angry? ______________

____

____

____

How did you express your anger? ______________________________________

____

____

____

How did others react to the way you expressed your anger? ________________

____

____

____

Was there a better way to express your anger? ____________________________

____

____

____

"In your anger do not sin" *(Ephesians 4:26).*

Bargaining

Dear God, Let's Make a Deal

Have you ever wanted to change something? We can change many things we do not like. We can change our hairstyle and our clothes. We can change the way we act and think. We can even change our friends. Some changes you can make on your own. Some changes you can only make with the help of your parent or another adult.

Name a change you would like to make? ________________________________

Can you make this change by yourself? ________________________________

When we want to change things and we need the help of others, we often bargain with them. We promise to do something to get them to do what we want them to do. Have you ever told a parent that you would do something like wash the dishes or clean the bathroom if they would let you go to the mall with your friend? Maybe you were a bit sneaky. Perhaps you did not say anything to your parent. You just started to do some work around the house and made sure you got on their good side before even asking. Then after they had complimented you, you said: "Oh, by the way, Jennifer and her family are going to the mall Friday night. They have invited me to go with them. Can I go?" You may not have thought about it, but you were making a bargain.

There are times in our hearts we bargain with God. God understands us. We cannot be sneaky with God because He knows what we are thinking even before we pray. Sometimes people promise God they will go to church, give Him their money, or become missionaries if He will just do something they want Him to do.

God has invited us to ask Him for what we need because He loves us. We can trust that He knows what is best. Sometimes God answers our prayers with a yes, and sometimes God answers our prayers with a no. Sometimes God's answer is wait. God may have to work several things out to answer our prayers. Whatever the answer is, we should thank Him and understand that He still loves us and is going to help us. Just remember, God always answers prayers.

It's a Real Bargain!

We bargain and compromise for things we want all the time. Think about how you would bargain in these situations.

Your mom packed you a good lunch. You have two pieces of fruit. While having lunch with your best friend, you notice that he has two cupcakes. You say ______________

____

____

Every other weekend you visit your dad. Next weekend it is your time to be with him. Your church group is going to have a camp out that weekend, and you really want to go. You call your dad on the phone and say ______________________

____

____

You really want to go to a movie with your friends, but you do not think your mother will let you go. Before you ask your mother, you decide you will try to get her in a good mood. You ______________________________

____

____

Can you think of other types of bargains you have made? Give us your own example.

____

____

Words to Know

Marriage—A legal contract between a man and woman. They promise to love, protect and take care of each other.

Divorce—A legal contract that ends the marriage contract of two married people.

Divorce Decree—Legal papers that a judge signs to make the divorce final. These papers will list all the details of the divorce.

Custody—A word used in a divorce decree to tell how the children will be taken care of until they become adults.

Custodial Parent—The parent who will primarily take care of the children. The children will live with this parent.

Non-Custodial Parent—The parent with whom the children do not live.

Visitation Rights—The rules in the divorce decree that describe when and under what conditions the children may spend time with the non-custodial parent.

Child Support—The money the non-custodial parent gives the custodial parent to help pay for the things the children need.

Sole Custody—Only one parent has the right to make decisions concerning the children. Sometimes the other parent can still visit the children, but he or she cannot make decisions for the children.

Joint Custody—Both parents share custody equally. There are three kinds of joint custody.

Joint Legal Custody—The children live with one parent, but both parents have equal rights to make decisions concerning the children.

Joint Physical Custody—The children take turns living with each parent, and both parents have to make all the decisions together concerning their children.

Joint Alternating Custody—The children take turns living with each parent. The parent whom the children are living with at the time is in charge of making decisions concerning the children.

Dear God,

Depression
Sometimes I Feel Sad

All people feel sad from time to time, but some people are sad all the time. Another word for being sad all the time is *depression*. In this session we are going to talk about sadness and depression. When we are sad, our mood and the way we behave changes.

Can you list three ways that your mood and the way you act change when you are sad?

1. ______________________________

2. ______________________________

3. ______________________________

Having sad feelings is normal when unhappy things happen. We may be sad when we lose something that we enjoy, like a bike or ball glove. We are also sad when we lose a pet. And we are very sad when someone we love dies.

When your parents became divorced, you lost having both of your parents live in the same house with you. You may have experienced other losses, too. You may have had to move from a house to an apartment. Maybe you had to change schools, and you miss your old friends and teachers. Sometimes you miss things like the furniture or pictures that used to be in your house. All these losses added together can make you feel sad.

The first year after the divorce is especially hard. On holidays, like Christmas and Thanksgiving, you wish your whole family was together, and this makes you feel sad. During that first year you will learn that life goes on. One day you will start to feel better.

Today we are going to
1. talk about times that we feel sad,
2. learn about ways that sad feelings affect our body,
3. discover what we can do for ourselves when we feel sad,
4. read Bible verses that teach us that God cares for us when we are feeling sad, and
5. pray and ask God to comfort us.

How We React to Depression

We can eat too much or too little food.

We have trouble thinking and concentrating.

We can sleep too much, or we can have a hard time falling asleep. We may even have nightmares often.

Things that used to interest us just do not seem interesting. We start feeling like everything is boring.

We feel like we do not have any energy.

We have headaches, stomachaches, or muscle aches all the time.

ACCEPTANCE
MOVING ON

Life is so exciting! There are so many wonderful things to do. If we stay depressed all the time, we will miss the great adventures ahead. Even when sad changes come into our lives, we still need to eat, sleep, go to school, and have fun. One day we may discover that we are not as sad as we used to be. When we discover that we can adjust, make some changes, and be satisfied, we are ready to move on with our lives. This stage of grief is called *acceptance.*

Acceptance does not mean we are suddenly happy or do not care anymore about the sad things that have happened. It means that we understand there are some things we cannot change. We need to learn to adjust to those things. There are some things that we *can* change. We need to find out what we *do* have the power to change and plan to make the changes we can. Start right now by making two lists. One list will be of things we cannot change, and the other will be a list of things we *do* have the power to change.

Things I Cannot Change	*Things I Can Change*
1. ______________________	1. ______________________
______________________	______________________
2. ______________________	2. ______________________
______________________	______________________
3. ______________________	3. ______________________
______________________	______________________
4. ______________________	4. ______________________
______________________	______________________
5. ______________________	5. ______________________
______________________	______________________

Knowing that God loves us will help us accept things that we cannot change. We can ask God to help us change the things that we have the power to change. It is good to know God cares.

Goals for Gina

Gina's parents are divorced. She and her mother moved to a new city where they could live closer to her mother's parents. At first Gina was angry and sad about the many changes in her life. She talked to her grandmother about her feelings. Her grandmother suggested that she list all the changes that were happening to her. Grandma suggested that Gina make one list of changes she could not do anything about and then make another list of changes that she could do something about.

Things I Cannot Change	*Things I Can Change*
1. The new city I live in.	1. Not having any friends in this city.
2. Not being able to see my dad very often.	2. The bedroom in my apartment.
3. Missing my old friends.	3. My communication with my dad.
4. Living in an apartment instead of a house.	4. My hairstyle.
5. My new school.	5. My church membership.

What Gina Decided to Do:

1. Gina realized that while she still does not know anyone her age in the new city, she can make new friends, especially when school starts.
2. Gina is sad because her new bedroom is not as pretty as her bedroom in the house where she used to live. Gina plans to ask her grandmother to help her decorate her new room.
3. Gina knows that she cannot see her dad except a few times a year. She has decided that she is going to be her dad's pen pal. She can be creative and think of different ways to keep communicating with her dad.
4. Her hair is long and straight. Her mother says she looks beautiful, but Gina is ready for a new look. Grandma suggests she look through magazines to find a new hairstyle that both she and her mother would like.
5. Gina misses her church where they lived. She and her mother plan to visit the church her grandparents attend. She knows they will be joining a new church family soon.

What About the Things Gina Could Not Change?

Gina looks over the list of the things she cannot change. She prays that God will help her to adjust to the things on this list. Gina is looking forward to working on the things that she can change. Her grandmother says change is just a part of life. Grandma should know; after all, she has lived a long time.

I Can Make Changes

List one thing you would like to change (one that you have the power to change or that others could help you change).

List some steps you could take to make this change possible.

1. ____

2. ____

3. ____

4. ____

5. ____

My Favorite Family Memory

Write about or draw a picture of something good your family did before your parents were divorced. If you cannot remember a time your parents lived together, tell or draw about a good family memory since the divorce.

It is good to remember the great times we had with our family.

God Helps Me Today

Practical Questions

Whom Can I Trust?

Being able to trust people is important. Many children, whose parents have divorced, have a difficult time trusting others. Before the divorce happened, you believed that your parents would always be together. You trusted your parents to keep your family together. Marriage is a very important trust relationship. A man and a woman promise to care for each other forever. Your parents did not keep that promise. Something happened, and they were divorced. You may feel sad that they broke an important promise to each other and to you.

Maybe you have trusted a friend with a very important secret, and they blabbed it all over the school. This may have left you feeling hurt. Trusting people is risky. They may disappoint you. They may reject you and make you feel hurt. Each time someone you trust disappoints you, it may be harder for you to trust other people again.

To feel close to our family and friends, we must trust. Maybe you need to learn to trust again. How can we learn to trust?

1. We need to learn to be a person that other people can trust.

2. We need to learn to talk to people who have hurt us and let them know how we feel. Sometimes we think that talking to them will make us feel worse, but it usually helps us to feel better.

3. We need to forgive other people when they disappoint us. Someday we will want other people to forgive us.

You can have wonderful friendships if you are willing to trust others. Learning to trust and forgive others will make all the difference.

Even though people disappoint us, the good news is that God can always be trusted.

"Let us hold unswervingly to the hope we profess, for he who promised is faithful" *(Hebrews 10:23).*

FIND THE QUALITIES THAT BUILD TRUST

These nine words describe a person who can be trusted. Look for these words in the box below and circle them.

dependable	honest	understanding	caring	truthful
believable	loving	confidential	consistent	

E G K A H T R U T H F U L Z C

C B E L I E V A B L E F T M E

O L F Q V S F C A K Q U R J U

N S W I R X H O N E S T D P O

S D G D V D I N B E B Y W A X

I O N E H I R F E Q D E Z T O

S W B P C F I I J O F P D E L

T J Q E D H J D V T P A U M O

E P N N Y N U E M X B K V H V

N A Q D G Z M N Y S C G I Z I

T V K A H D R T L C J K J L N

B E S B G B Y I K U N O R I G

C F C L L N C A R I N G T A Y

Z L X E G L M L M X T W H T S

U N D E R S T A N D I N G R N

Would other people use these words to describe you?

Trust Busters

You share a problem you are having with a friend at school. You ask them to please not tell anyone. Before the day is up, you find out your other friends know all about your problem.

One way you could react is: ______________________________

____

Your dad and mom are divorced. You live with your dad. Your mom is supposed to have you every other weekend. She has found many new friends since the divorce. You call her and check on your weekend plans. She says she is coming to get you. Friday after school you get ready for her to pick you up. It gets later and later. You try to reach her at home and no one answers. Later, you find out she went out with some friends.

One way you could react is: ______________________________

____

You ask your aunt some questions about your family. Your aunt loves you and feels that the answers to your questions might make you sad. She gives you an answer she thinks is better. Later, you find out that what she said is not exactly true.

One way you could react is: ______________________________

____

When you are with your dad, he says things about your mother that are not nice. When you get back home, your mother questions you about your dad. You know they do not trust each other. They are making it hard for you to know which one to trust.

One way you could react is: ______________________________

____

Am I To Blame?

We are responsible only for what we do. Often people have guilty feelings about things they did not do. For example, some children think their parents' divorce is their fault because they misbehaved or made bad grades. Maybe the only times they heard their parents argue was about them, so they think surely the divorce was their fault.

Do you feel like your parents' divorce was your fault? ____________________________

Divorce is an adult problem. There is nothing a child can do that can cause his parents to choose to get a divorce. All children make their parents mad or disappointed at some time, but that is not why their parents divorced. Divorce happens when parents have serious problems with each other.

Children who think that the divorce is their fault are experiencing FALSE GUILT. We experience FALSE GUILT when we feel guilty, but we have not done anything to make us feel that way.

REAL GUILT is the feeling we have when we have really done something wrong.

After we do something wrong, we need to:

- ♡ ask God to forgive us.
- ♡ decide not to do this wrong thing again.
- ♡ ask the person we hurt to forgive us.
- ♡ try to fix the situation.
- ♡ forgive ourselves.
- ♡ learn from the experience.
- ♡ stop blaming ourselves and feeling bad.

Guilty or Not . . . But Here I Am!

Real Guilt—describes the unhappy feelings we have when we know we have done something wrong.

False Guilt—are feelings of guilt when you have not really done anything wrong.

	Guilty	*Not Guilty*
Your mom is in a bad mood. She starts yelling at you for no reason at all. You are confused and think you did something to make her act this way.	________	________
You and a friend are playing a board game, and you are the banker. You know that you are loosing. While your friend is not looking, you take some money out of the bank. Later, you win the game, but you really do not feel good about it.	________	________
You are trying to help your dad in the yard. You pick weeds out of a flower bed. Later, you find out that you mistook the real young plants for weeds and pulled them out. Are you guilty?	________	________
You get angry with a girl at school. You try to get her in trouble. Your plan works. Later, you feel guilty. Are you to blame?	________	________
Your dad moves out of the house. You feel very sad. You keep thinking of times you bothered him by making too much noise. You start to feel guilty. Was his moving out your fault?	________	________

The Shoulda, Coulda, Woulda, What If Trap

Read the blame statement in each trap. Write down who was blamed for the divorce.

If Mom **coulda** not yelled all the time, dad **woulda** not have left home.

*Blamed*____________________________

I **shoulda** kept my room cleaner and not made so much noise and my parents **woulda** not fought about my behavior so much.

*Blamed*____________________________

What if my dad had not gotten laid off from his job? I'm sure all the fights between my parents started after dad was laid off.

*Blamed*____________________________

If dad **woulda** come home from work earlier every day, mom **woulda** not filed for divorce.

*Blamed*____________________________

If God **woulda** answered my prayers, we **coulda** still been a family.

*Blamed*____________________________

My parents were okay until they started spending time with other friends. If my mom **woulda** not spent so much time with her friends, we **woulda** not been in this mess!

*Blamed*____________________________

What Would You Do If . . . ?

A person came to the door and told you they were a repair person and wanted you to open the door.

You were home alone, and someone called your house and asked to speak to your parent.

You arrived home and discovered you had lost your key.

You were at home alone and a stranger knocked at the door.

8 9 1 1 2 5 4 7 6

What are some important phone numbers to know?

You were at home alone and got hungry.

What If My Parents Date or Remarry?

When adults date, they spend a lot of time with each other. Spending time together helps them get to know each other. After a man and woman date for a while, they may develop special feelings for each other. They may begin to care for and love each other. They could decide to get married. If your natural parent remarries, the new adult in your parent's life will be your stepparent. Perhaps you already have a stepfather or stepmother.

My stepmother's name is ______________________________

My stepfather's name is______________________________

It will take time to get used to new people in your family. New situations in your families can be scary and exciting at the same time. Fill in the blanks below with why you think that having a new stepparent can be scary and exciting.

Having a new stepparent can be scary because...

1. ______________________________
2. ______________________________
3. ______________________________
4. ______________________________

Having a new stepparent can be exciting because...

1. ______________________________
2. ______________________________
3. ______________________________
4. ______________________________

Today we are going to talk about parents dating and remarrying. We will role-play talking to natural parents about the feelings you may have about their dating and remarrying.

It's Great to Communicate

Your parents are smart, but they cannot read your mind. When you are upset about one of your parents dating or remarrying, you need to talk to that parent about your feelings.

When we talk about tough subjects, HOW we say what we are feeling is as important as WHAT we say. When we are upset, it is easy for us to express our feelings in ways that make the other person feel badly. Instead of helping our relationship with them, we can make it worse.

"You" Statements vs. "I" Statements

Problem—Billy misses spending time with his dad. He can give his dad this message in 2 ways.

"You" statement—Billy can tell his dad how he feels in a way that blames and accuses his dad.

Example—"Dad, YOU don't spend time with me anymore. You just spend time with your silly girlfriend."

"I" statement—Billy can tell his dad how he feels without blaming anyone.

Example—"Dad, I miss not spending time with you. Can we plan to do something this week?"

Communication Cartoons

Choose a problem and practice turning "You" statements into "I" statements. Fill in the balloon in each box as an example of communicating what you feel.

Problem #1 ______________________________

Problem #2 ______________________________

Why are "I" statements better than "You" statements?

How Can I Help My Family?

My Family - It Is One of a Kind!

All families are unique! Just like there is no one just like you; there is no family just like yours. There are five types of families that children live in. They are:

Nuclear Family—A father and mother and their biological children.

Single Parent Family—A father or mother and his or her biological children.

Blended Family—A parent and a stepparent who have children from another marriage. Sometimes only one parent has children. Sometimes both people have children. The brothers or sisters who belong to the stepparent are called your stepbrothers or stepsisters. If your parent and stepparent have a new baby, the baby is your half brother or half sister.

Adoptive Family—A father and mother who have permanent legal custody of a child who is not their biological child. Birth parents are called biological parents.

Foster Family—Adults who help care for children for part of their lives. They love, protect, and provide for the children just like they were their own children.

HELPING MY FAMILY

Listed below are jobs that every family needs to do. All these jobs are important. Some are harder than others. Who in your family does these jobs?

washes clothes ________________

cooks meals ________________

irons clothes ________________

vacuums ________________

mows the grass ________________

saves money ________________

takes care of children ________________

buys groceries ________________

dusts furniture ________________

pays bills ________________

makes bed ________________

folds clothes ________________

bathes the baby ________________

cleans the bathroom ________________

works in the yard ________________

washes dishes ________________

feeds the pet(s) ________________

goes to school ________________

does homework ________________

mops floors ________________

Is it fair for only one person to do all these jobs? ________________

If only one family member does all these jobs, NO wonder they might get tired and cranky! All members of the family need to help their family with the jobs they can.

What can you do for your family?

1. ________________
2. ________________
3. ________________
4. ________________
5. ________________
6. ________________

Problem Solving

Ask yourself these questions the next time you have a problem you need to solve.

1. What is the problem? ______________________________

2. Is this problem solvable?

Yes

No  Learn to adjust to your situation

3. Can I solve this problem?

Yes

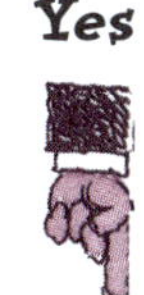

No

4. What are my choices?

A. ______________________________

B. ______________________________

C. ______________________________

5. Who can help me?

A. ______________________________

B. ______________________________

C. ______________________________

6. What is the best choice for me? ______________________________

7. Do it!

8. Think it over. Did my plan work?

Yes

REJOICE!

No

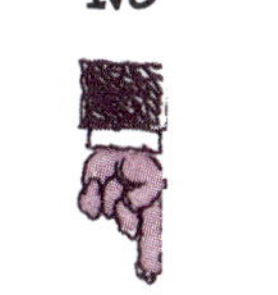

TRY AGAIN!

Bible Leaders Came From All Five Types of Families

Match the Bible Character with his family type.

Nuclear Family •	• Moses was adopted by Pharaoh's daughter when he was only a baby. God led the princess to choose Moses' own mother to help her care for Moses. Later, the Princess gave Moses a good education. God used Moses to lead His people to their promise land.
Single Parent Family •	• Samuel was raised by the priest Eli. Samuel's mother gave him to priest Eli to raise and use Samuel to serve in the temple. Samuel was an Old Testament leader.
Blended Family •	• Timothy had a Christian mother who taught him about God. His father was a man from Greece. Timothy helped Paul with his missionary work.
Adoptive Family •	• Solomon was a king who was known for being fair and wise. His father was King David and mother was Bathsheba. Solomon had many half-brothers and half-sisters.
Foster Family •	• King Josiah became a king when he was just eight years old because his father died. Josiah was a good king. The Bible says that he did what was right in the eyes of God.

God blesses and uses people who put their trust in him.

How Do I Cope With My Painful Feelings?

Sometimes things happen to us that really hurt.

- ♡ A broken promise.
- ♡ A lie told about us.
- ♡ Not getting the attention we want from someone we love.
- ♡ Being treated unfairly.

Our feelings about these things are important. We cannot pretend our feelings are not real!

It helps me to forgive when I:

- ♡ Talk to the person who hurt my feelings and let him know in "I" statements how I feel.
- ♡ Hear the other person apologize for hurting my feelings.
- ♡ Let some time pass by.
- ♡ Ask God to help me want to forgive.

When I choose to forgive:

- ♡ I understand that I am not perfect and will need someone to forgive me someday.
- ♡ I help myself feel better inside.
- ♡ I have better friendships with other people.
- ♡ I obey God.

THE MESSENGER "NOT"

1. Give an example of a message your mother asked you to give to your dad.

____

____

2. Give an example of a message your dad wanted you to give to your mother.

____

____

Carrying messages may make you feel you are taking sides. You may feel afraid you are going to make one parent angry. It can make you feel you are caught in the middle of your parents' problems.

Review what you learned in Session 9 about "I" statements and "You" statements. Using an "I" statement, what could you have said to the parent who wanted you to carry the message you wrote above?

1. Mom, ____

____

____

2. Dad, ____

____

____

I Know God Loves Me

God's plan for families is that they learn to care for each other. One of the ways that we care for one another is by saying nice things to the people we love.

Everyone Wants Love and Approval

Things People Want to Hear:	*I Would Like This Said to Me By:*	*I Can Say This to:*
You are so smart.		
I love you.		
You did a great job.		
You look great.		
I think you are special.		
(You fill in the blank!)		

It is NOT in our power to make people say nice things to us.
It IS in our power to say nice things to other people.

Reach Out and Help Others

You have learned many new skills through KidShare. You have learned from your problems. When you meet children who have other problems or whose parents are divorced, you will be able to help them.

You can:

♡ Listen to their story.
♡ Share your story with them.
♡ Help them think of solutions to their problems.
♡ Pray for them.

Practice Thinking of Ways to Help

1. If Joe is new in school and does not have friends, I could ______________________

   ____

2. If Abigail is quiet and cries all the time, I could ______________________

   ____

3. If Andrew's parents just told him they were getting a divorce, I could __________

   ____

4. If Maria is angry because she has not seen her dad in over a year and he forgot

   her birthday, I could ____

   ____

5. If Kim's parents are divorced and she keeps saying she does not care anyway,

   I could ____

   ____

My Anger Diary

	Date	*What Made Me Angry*	*How I Reacted*
1.			
2.			
3.			
4.			
5.			
6.			
7.			

Given out at the end of Session 2 – for Session 3 assignment

KidShare Weekly At Home Assignments

Assignment for Session 6

Think of something that you really enjoy doing. This activity has to be something that will be possible for you to do this week. Tell the group what you really enjoy doing and write that activity on the back of this card. Next week, plan to share what you did for fun. If you can, bring your pleasure activity to show and tell. For example, if you like to play a musical instrument, bring your musical instrument and play for us.

Assignment for Session 3

On the sheet, "My Anger Diary," that we provided, keep a diary of times you felt angry this week. Think about what happened to cause you to feel angry. Next, write down what you did when you were angry. Write these answers in the space provided. Be sure to bring your sheet back with you next week.

Assignment for Session 5

Read the Scripture verse printed on your "My Scripture is ________" worksheet. Write the verse on the back of this card. Read the verse everyday. Think about these questions:

1. What does this verse mean?
2. How does this verse make you feel?
3. How can this verse help you when you feel sad?

Discuss this verse and these questions with your parent or another adult. Plan to share what you learned in your group meeting.

Assignment for Session 2

Ask your parents for some old magazines you can use to cut out pictures. Go through the magazines and find pictures of people's faces showing the following feelings: joy, anger, love, fear, and sadness. Bring as many pictures as you can find. We are going to use these pictures to make a montage.

Assignment for Session 4

Talk to your parents about their custody agreement of you in the divorce decree. Ask your parents what is the legal name of their custody agreement for you. Write the legal name on the back of this card and bring it with you when you come to Session 4. Ask your parents to explain what their custody arrangements are.

Assignment for Session 1

Look through pictures of yourself. Choose five pictures to bring to the group session next week. These pictures should help us get to know you.

Assignment for Session 12

Think back on all that you have learned in the past twelve weeks. List on the back of this card three of the most important things you have learned from being in this support group. Be prepared to share at least one of these items in our group meeting next week.

Assignment for Session 11

Interview your parent or another adult on the subject of forgiveness. Ask the following questions:

1. What does *forgive* mean?
2. Why is it sometimes hard to forgive people?
3. What can we do to show we have forgiven someone?

Be sure and take notes. Bring your answers to the next group session.

Assignment for Session 10

Think of three things that you can do this week that will help your family get along better. List these three things on the back of this card. Do at least one of these things this week. Be ready to share with the group what you did and how it helped your family get along better.

Assignment for Session 9

Draw a picture of what you would consider to be the best thing that could happen to your family now. This picture could include a new stepparent and stepbrothers and sisters, or it may just be a picture of what your family is like right now. You can add things you would like your family to have, like a cat, or a dog, a new house, or a new car. Draw whatever you wish. Bring your drawing to the next support-group session.

Assignment for Session 8

Have a discussion with your parent and one other adult. Ask them to explain the difference between real guilt and false guilt. Think of an example of real guilt and an example of false guilt to share with the group next time we meet. Be sure to make notes of your answers and examples.

Assignment for Session 7

Think about the character qualities that you would like in a best friend. Talk to your parent about qualities they think are important for people to have. On the back of this card, list these character qualities. Bring your list with you next week. We will talk about the qualities a person we can trust should have.